I0407418

Disclaimer

The information provided within this eBook is for general informational purposes only. While we try to keep the information up-to-date and correct, there are no representations or warranties, express or implied, about the completeness, accuracy, reliability, suitability or availability with respect to the information, products, services, or related graphics contained in this eBook for any purpose.

©Mumbai

General Knowledge and Awareness Questions (India) - Almost For All Competitive Exams!!

Table of Contents

Questions part A

1. Who is the Chairman of NITI Aayog?

a) Arvind Panagariya

b) Dr. Vijay Kelkar

c) Sunil Kanoria

d) Anupam Srivastava

e) Narendra Modi

2. In Strategic alliance, the alliance partners?

a) Merge with each other

b) One partner acquires the other

c) Remain separate entities

d) One partner amalgamates with other

e) None of the above

3. The premium on accident insurance under PMJDY will be borne by?

a) National Payments Corporation of India

b) Life Insurance Corporation of India

c) General Insurance Corporation of India

d) Central Government

e) None of these

4. INFINET is set up in which of the following cities?

a) Mumbai

b) New Delhi

c) Hyderabad

d) Chennai

e) Kolkata

5. The essential characteristic of whatever serves as money is that it must:

a) Be issued by the State

b) Be generally acceptable

c) Cannot be wholly fiduciary

d) Have some intrinsic value

e) None of these

6. Digital India Programme is planned to be fully implemented by:

a) 2016

b) 2017

c) 2018

d) 2019

e) 2020

7. Under Pradhan Mantri Sneh Bandhan Yojana, an individual may invest an amount of:

a) Rs. 5000

b) Rs. 5001

c) Rs. 5005

d) Rs. 5010

e)Rs. 6001

8. What is the Credit guarantee corpus amount of MUDRA Bank?

a) Rs. 3000 crores

b) Rs. 4000 crores

c) Rs. 2500 crores

d) Rs. 2000 crores

e) Rs. 1500 crores

9. The principal liability of a Bank relates to ___:

a) it's investment abroad

b) it's investment at home

c) repayment of it's customer's deposits

d) it's requirements to make special deposits when requested

e) None of these

10. Which of the following is not a function of the Commercial Bank?

a) Acting as a lender of last resort

b) Lending to the private and public sectors

c) The provision of a cheque system for setting debts

d) The provision of safe deposit facilities

e) None of these

11. Under Pradhan Mantri Jeevan Jyoti Bima Yojana, the life insurance cover is for how many years:

a) 1 year

b) 2 years

c) 3 years

d) 4 years

e) 5 years

12. As per Pradhan Mantri Suraksha Bima Yojana (PMSBY), if the customer has taken a cover under

multiple bank accounts then the amount of premium under this will be:

a) Forfeited

b) Renewed

c) Double

d) Same

e) None of the above

13. Digital India Programme is centered on 3 key vision areas. Which of the following is not

included in these vision areas?

a) Digital Infrastructure as a core utility to every citizen

b) Governance and services on demand

c) To promote digital banking

d) Digital Empowerment of citizens

e) None of the above

14. A customer does not require a bank account to obtain ___:

a) a loan

b) a cheque book

c) a banker's draft

d) an overdraft

e) None of these

15. Atal Pension Yojana (APY) offers fixed amount of pension ranging between Rs. 1000 to ___

depending upon the contribution which will be based on the age of joining the APY:

a) Rs. 2000

b) Rs. 3000

c) Rs. 4000

d) Rs. 5000

e) Rs. 6000

16. Which of the following is not the function of RBI?

a) Issue of currency notes

b) Maintaining financial stability

c) Subsidies to people

d) Banker to Bank

e) Banker to Government

17. Which of the following documents are required for registration of a Jeevan Pramaan?

a) Aadhar Number

b) PPO number

c) Bank Account Number

d) All of the above

e) None of the above

18. As per Sukanya Samriddhi Account the tenure of deposit is for ___ years from the date of opening of the account:

a) 15 years

b) 20 years

c) 21 years

d) 24 years

e) 25 years

19. Under Sukanya Samriddhi Account (SSA), the bank account will be opened for a girl child upto the age of ____:

a) 5 years

b) 8 years

c) 10 years

d) 15 years

e) 12 years

20. What is the initial corpus of MUDRA Bank?

a) Rs. 20,000 crores

b) Rs. 30,000 crores

c) Rs. 35,000 crores

d) Rs. 40,000 crores

e) Rs. 25,000 crores

21. In India national income is estimated by?

a) Finance Commission

b) Central Statistical Organisation

c) Planning Commission

d) Finance Ministry

e) Reserve Bank of India

22. A scheme named _____ offers a long term subscription to Pradhan Mantri Suraksha Bima Yojana with attached Fixed Deposit.

a) Suraksha Deposit Scheme

b) Suraksha Insurance Cover

c) Jeevan Suraksha Yojana

d) Suraksha Cover

e) Suraksha Investment Scheme

23. What is/are the objective of Pradhan Mantri Kaushal Vikas Yojana (PMKVY)?

a) To impart skill training to youth

b) Focus on first time entrants to the labour market

c) Focus on class 10 and class 12 dropouts

d) All of these

e) None of the above

24. What is meant by "Underwriting", the term frequently used in financial sector?

a) Under valuation of the assets

b) The Act of taking on a risk

c) Giving a Guarantee that a loan will not become a bad loan

d) Assignment of Insurance Policy

e) Hypothecation of stocks

25. Misery Index' represents?

a) Sum of rate of inflation and rate of unemployment

b) Product of rate of inflation and rate of unemployment

c) Proportion of very poor to poor living below the poverty line

d) Inflation rate divided by unemployment rate

e) Both (b) and (c)

26. Which of the following statement is true for IMF?

a) It is not an agency of UNO

b) It can grant loan to any country of the world

c) It can grant loan to state Govt. of a country

d) It grants loan only to member nations

e) It can grant loan only to European Countries

27. Which pair is not correct?

a) EXIM Bank Financing

for export import

b) RBI Banker's

bank

c) IDBI Industrial

finance

d) FCI Financial

Assistance to Commercial Banks

e) NABARD Apex

organization for assisting Agriculture & Rural Development

28. Statutory Liquidity Ratio (SLR) of commercial banks means:

a) The percentage of cash that banks keep with them, as per IBA Guidelines

b) A portion of Fixed Deposits to be maintained with RBI as per RBI Act 1934

c) Every bank is required to maintain a proportion of their Net Demand and Time Liabilities as

liquid assets in the form of cash, gold and unencumbered

approved securities

d) The rate at which central bank of the country (in India it is RBI) allows finance to commercial

banks

e) None of the above

29. Which bank is created for the promotion of cross border trade and investment?

a) NABARD

b) SIDBI

c) EXIM Bank

d) IDBI

e) None of the above

30. "Closed Economy" is that economy in which?

Which of the following is not a fertilizer mineral?

(a) Nitrate

(b) Phosphate

(c)Tungsten

(d) Potash

(*Ans : *c)

What is the minimum capital requirement for New Banks in the Private Sector?

a) Rs.200 crore

 b) Rs. 300 crore

c) Rs. 500 crore

d) Rs. 600 crore

e) None ...

A process of preparing a floppy diskette for use is called

1) assembling

2) translating

3) parsing

4) formatting

5)None

31. Apna Sahakari Bank Ltd is located at?

a) Bhopal, Madhya Pradesh

b) Kolkata, West Bengal

c) Lucknow, Uttar Pradesh

d) Mumbai, Maharashtra

e) Hyderabad, Telangana

32. On which of the following types of cheques alterations are not allowed by RBI?

a) Paper cheque

b) CTS cheque

c) Electronic cheque

d) Cheque with account payee crossing

e) None of the above

33. What is the income criteria for sanctioning loan under Prime minister Employment

Generation Programme (PMEGP)?

a) Rs. 18,000 per head

b) Rs. 18,000 per family

c) Rs. 24,000 per family

d) Rs. 36,000 per family

e) No ceiling on Income

34. Under Negotiable Instruments Act1881

Inchoate Instrument means:

a) Invalid instrument

b) Incomplete instrument

c) Restricts further endorsement

d) Illegal Instrument

e) None of the above

35. To apply the Garnishee Order, the Banker Customer

relationship should be:

a) Creditor Debtor

b) Agent Principal

c) Trustee Beneficiary

d) Debtor Creditor

e) None of the above

36. Under Pradhan Mantri Suraksha Bima Yojana (PMSBY) insurance cover for accidental death

or permanent full disability is:

a) Rs. 2 lakhs

b) Rs. 3 lakhs

c) Rs. 4 lakhs

d) Rs. 5 lakhs

e) Rs. 1 lakh

37. In term deposits if the Principal and Interest is Rs. 20,000 or above it should not be paid in

cash as per _____:

a) RBI Act

b) Negotiable Instruments Act

c) Banking Regulation Act

d) Income tax Act

e) None of the above

38. As per BCSBI Banking

Codes and Standard Board of India, duplicate DD should be issued

within ___ from the date of request?

a) 7 days

b) 14 days

c) 10 days

d) 15 days

e) 3 days

ANSWERS part a:
1) e 2) c 3) a 4) c 5) b 6) d 7) b 8) a 9) c 10) a

11) a 12) a 13) c 14) c 15) d 16) c 17) d 18) c 19) c 20) a

21) b 22) a 23) d 24) b 25) a 26) d 27) d 28) c 29) c 30) a

31) d 32) b 33) e 34) b 35) d 36) a 37) d 38) b

Questions Part B
1. RBI updated KYC norms on 2 September 2016. In this context, KYC stands for ......

1) Know Your Copy

2) Know Your Custom

3) Know Your Customer

4) Know Your Credential

5) Know Your Cashier

2. Which of the following statement is correct regarding KYC?

1) KYC is a process by which banks obtain information about the identity and address of the customers.

2) KYC procedure is to be completed by the banks while opening accounts.

3) Banks required periodically update their customers' KYC details.

4) KYC process helps to ensure that banks' services are not misused.

5) All of above

3. As per RBI update rules of KYC, what are the KYC requirements for opening a bank account?

1) Proof of identity

2) Proof of address

3) Recent photograph

4) None of them required

5) All of above required

4. Which of the following documents is not one of the 'proof of identity' in KYC as per RBI directions?

1) PAN Card

2) Aadhar Card

3) Birth Chart issued by famous Astrologer

4) NREGA Job Card

5) Voters' Identity Card

5. Government of India has notified six documents as OVDs for the purpose of producing proof of identity. In this context, OVD stands for ......

1) Officially Voter Documents

2) Officially Valid Documents

3) Officially Void Documents

4) One Valid Documents

5) Over Valid Documents

6. If any person does not have any of the listed documents named as 'proof of identity', whether that person can open a bank account?

1) No, he cannot open account.

2) Yes, he can open account and after 10 days he can submit Identity Proof.

3) Yes, the customer can open account in RBI, as RBI can give current account to individuals effective from 1 July 2016.

4) Yes, he can still open a bank account known as 'Small Account' by submitting recent photograph and putting signature or thumb impression in the presence of the bank official.

5) Yes, by taking special permission from State Government.

7. Usually Small Accounts will have limitations. As per the limitations, at any point of time, the maximum balance in the account should not exceed ....

1) Rs.50,000

2) Rs.1,00,000

3) Rs.1,000

4) Rs.10,00,000

5) Rs.75,000

8. Total credits in one year should not exceed .... in Small Accounts as per the order of RBI.

1) Rs.10,00,000

2) Rs.8,00,000

3) Rs.1,000

4) Rs.5,00,000

5) Rs.1,00,000

9. In the Small Accounts, total withdrawal and transfers in a month should not exceed ....

1) Rs.1000

2) Rs.20,000

3) Rs.50,000

4) Rs.10,000

5) Rs.1,00,000

10. Whether Foreign remittances can be credited in Small Accounts?

1) Yes, but up to $ 1000 per month

2) Yes, but up to $ 50 per month

3) No

4) Yes

5) None of above option correct

11. Small Accounts remain operational initially for a period of .... if the customer does not provide any of the valid documents and thereafter, for a further period of 12 months if the holder of such an account provides evidence to the bank of having applied for any of the officially valid documents.

1) 6 months

2) 3 months

3) 18 months

4) 12 months

5) 24 months

12. Which of the following document cannot be produced as Proof of Address (PoA) as per the updated KYC rules?

1) Utility bill, which is not more than two months old, of any service provider (electricity, telephone, water bill etc).

2) Bank account or Post Office savings bank account statement.

3) Any hotel bill proved staying of 3 days.

4) Property or Municipal Tax receipt.

5) Documents issued by Government departments of foreign jurisdictions or letter issued by Foreign Embassy or Mission in India.

13. Banks required to categorise their customers based on risk assessment in three categories as per depending on their AML risk assessment as per the RBI directions. These three

categories are ....

1) Rich, Poor and Middle Class People

2) Low, Medium and High

3) Brown, Black and Red

4) A, B and C

5) Territorial, Extra Territorial and None

14. eKYC

refers to electronic KYC. eKYC

is possible only for those who have Aadhaar

numbers. Aadhar Card issued by Unique Identification Authority of India (UIDAI). Who was

appointed as the parttime

Chairman of UIDAI on 8 September 2016?

1) U.K.Sinha

2) T.S. Vijayan

3) Devendra Sikri

4) Alka Sirohi

5) J. Satyanarayana

15. APB implemented by National Payments Corporation of India (NPCI), which uses Aadhaar

number as a central key for electronically channelizing the Government subsidies and benefits.

APB stands for ....

1) Aadhaar Payment Bridge

2) Aadhaar Point Bridge

3) Aadhaar pool Bridge

4) Aadhaar Payment Book

5) Aadhaar Payment Brand

16. As per the order of RBI, KYC exercise needs to be done for all those who want to make

domestic remittances of .... and above and all foreign remittances.

1) Rs.50,000

2) Rs.5,00,000

3) Rs.10,000

4) Rs.1,000

5) Rs.5,000

17. Banks can close the account of customer, if customer does not provide the KYC documents at the time of periodic updation. Before closing the account, the bank may, however, impose 'partial freezing', Banks have to give due notice of three month sand reminder for further period of ....

1) Six months

2) Three months

3) Two months

4) Ten months

5) Eight months

18. Which bank has bagged four awards for inclusive insurance for 2016 from Skoch Group?

1) Telangana Gramin Bank

2) Puduvai Bharathiyar Grama Bank

3) Karnataka Vikas Grameena Bank

4) Andhra Pradesh Gramin Vikas Bank

5) Pradhama Gramin Bank

19. India signed MoU with African Development Bank (AfDB) Group to host the next annual meetings at Mahatma Gandhi Convention Centre, Ahmedabad from 22nd May to 26th May 2017. Where is the head quarter of African Development Bank (AfDB) Group?

1) Algiers (Algeria)

2) Cairo (Egypt)

3) Port Louis (Mauritius)

4) Abidjan (Ivory Coast)

5) Victoria (Seychelles)

20. In which year, African Development Bank (AfDB) was established?

1)1945

2) 1966

3) 2015

4) 1964

5) 2016

21. How many member nations are there in African Development Bank (AfDB)?

1) 189

2) 67

3) 78

4) 57

5) 5

22. Who is the Nigerian National is the present head of African Development Bank (AfDB)?

1) Jim Yong Kim

2) Take Hiko Nakao

3) Akinwumi Adesina

4) Jin Liquin

5) K V Kamath

23. Which scheme recently notified to offer financial incentives to employers on 1 September 2016?

1) National Apprenticeship Policy Scheme.

2) National Appendix Promotion Scheme.

3) National Apprenticeship Promotion Scheme.

4) National Apprenticeship Price Scheme.

5) Ninth Apprenticeship Promotion Scheme.

24. Under National Apprenticeship Promotion Scheme (NAPS), an outlay of Rs.10,000 crore

granted with a target of 50 lakh apprentices to be trained by ......

1) 201920

2) 201819

3) 202122

4) 202425

5) 201718

25. Indian Railway will provide insurance cover up to 10 lakh rupees for passengers travelling on eticket

after paying a premium of ...

1) Rs.1

2) 25 paise

3) Rs.2

4) 92 paisa

5) Rs.5

26. For insuring its passengers, the Indian Railways selected three insurance companies. They

are Shriram General Insurance, ICICI Lombard General Insurance and ......

1) Royal Sundaram General Insurance

2) LIC

3) Max Bhupa Health Insurance

4) HDFC Ergo

5) Bajaj Allianz

27. Nadia Murad Basee Taha appointed as UN Goodwill Ambassador for the Dignity of

Survivors of Human Trafficking of the UN Office on Drugs and Crime (UNODC). She belongs to

....

1) Pakistan

2) Afghanistan

3) Syria

4) Iraq

5) Lebanon

28. United Nations Office on Drugs and Crime (UNODC) was established in ....

1) 1997

2) 1945

3) 1946

4) 1964

5) 1972

29. Under Vanbandhu Kalyan Yojna scheme, Rs.4,800 crore funded irrigation and drinking water supply projects in tribal areas of .... launched by PM on 17 September 2016.

1) Gujarat

2) Assam

3) Chhattisgarh

4) AP

5) Tamilnadu

30. World Economic Freedom Index 2016 declared. Indiaís rank in this index stood at....

1) 100

2) 120

3) 112

4) 10

5) 32

31. Which scheme was launched to support and promote organic farming and thereby improving soil health? The Scheme encourages farmers to adopt ecofriendly

concept of cultivation and

reduce their dependence on fertilizers and agricultural chemicals to improve yields.

1) The Pradhan Mantri Fasal Bima Yojana

2) eNAM

3) Paramaparagat Krishi Vikas Yojana

4) Pradhan Mantri Krishi Sinchai Yojana

5) Kisan Vikas Patra

32. As per latest RBI report, which state has topped in attracting industrial investments in 201516

with an investment of Rs 21,914 crore out of the Rs 1,38,700 crore Gross Investments

across India?

1) Andhra Pradesh

2) Gujarat

3) Maharashtra

4) Tamil nadu

5) Karnataka

33. Who headed the committee that was constituted to look into the alternatives to pellet guns

to disperse crowd?

1) Madhukar Guphta

2) Traun Ramadorai

3) TVSN Prasad

4) Ratan P watal

5) P.K.Sinha

34. Theme of the 'International Day for the Preservation of the Ozone Layer' 2016 is....

1) Ozone and climate: Returned by a world united

2) 'Ozone and Atmosphere: Restored by a world united'

3) 'Ozone and Oxygen: Restored by a world united'

4) 'Ozone and climate: Targeted by a world united'

5) 'Ozone and climate: Restored by a world united'

35. Water Resources Ministry and Agriculture Ministry on 16 September 2016 made MoU to

develop organic farming in over 5000 villages along the banks of .... river in each Gram

Panchayat representing a cluster under Paramaparagat Krishi Vikas Yojana.

1) Godavari

2) Krishna

3) Ganga

4) Kaveri

5) Narmada

Answers Part B:

13,

25,

35,

43,

52,

64,

71,

85,

94,

103

114,

123,

132,

145,

151,

161,

172,

183,

194,

204

213,

223,

233,

241,

254,

261,

274,

281,

291,

303

313,

321,

333,

345,

353

Questions Part C

1. Who is appointed as the 24th Governor of the Reserve Bank of India in place of Mr.

Raghuram Rajan?

a) H.R. Khan

b) N.S. Vishwanathan

c) R. Gandhi

d) S.S. Mundra

e) Urjit Patel

2. Which is the other bank that will be merged with SBI besides its five subsidiary banks?

a) City Union Bank

b) Karur Vysya Bank

c) South Indian Bank

d) Bharatiya Mahila Bank

e) IDBI

3. Which of the following products launched by most of the banks help farmers in getting instant credit for various agricultural purposes?

a) Kisan Credit Card

b) Personal loan

c) Business loan

d) Only (a) and (b)

e) None of the above

4. Banks have started opening biometric ATMs now. Such ATMs will prove most beneficial for which of the following categories of customers?

a) Govt. employees

b) HNIs

c) NRIs

d) Students

e) Illiterate people

5. Which of the following institution provides long run finance to industries?

a) UTI

b) LIC

c) GIC

d) IDBI

e) All of the above

6. In banking terminology the word "Co obligant"

means:

a) A person who has guaranteed the account of another person(s)

b) A person who has executed an indemnity bond in a bank's favour

c) A person who has assumed obligations of contract jointly with other person(s)

d) A person/ business undertaking opening a documentary letter of credit

e) None of the above

7. Which of following is the first such company of the country which offers services for the resolution of Non performing

assets upon acquisition from bankers?

a) CIBIL

b) ARCIL

c) ECGC

d) CRISIL

e) IDFC

8. Who among the following has been appointed as Executive Director of the RBI, replacing N.S.

Vishwanathan, who recently was elevated as Deputy Governor of the RBI?

a) M.D. Patra

b) Sudharshan Sen

c) Chandan Sinha

d) U.S. Paliwal

e) Deepali Pant Joshi

9. Account payee crossing is a direction of the drawer:

a) to collecting banker

b) to drawee banker

c) to payee

d) to all endorsees

e) paying Banker

10. Govt. proposes to do away the ___ for its fiscal affairs management from fiscal 201718.

a) Plan and Non Plan

classification

b) Revenue receipts and Capital receipts classification

c) Tax and non tax receipts classification

d) Only (a) and (b)

e) None of these

11. The advantages of securitization for a Bank is:

a) It provides liquidity to the issuing Bank

b) The Bank capital does not get blocked

c) Securitization proceeds can be used for fresh lending

d) Only (a) and (b)

e) (a), (b) and (c)

12. Example of the product line of a

Bank is:

a) Car loan b) Personal loan

c) Home loan

d) Mortgage loan

e) All of the above

13. As per Prevention of Money Laundering act, the banks are required to maintain record of transactions for a minimum period of ____ from date of cessation of the transaction.

a) 2 years

b) 5 years

c) 10 years

d) 20 years

e) 25 years

14. Statutory cash reserve ratio for scheduled banks is regulated by Reserve Bank of India under powers conferred upon it by?

a) Reserve Bank of India act, 1934

b) Banking Regulation act, 1949

c) Companies act, 1956

d) Union Ministry of Finance

e) Negotiable Instruments act, 1881

15. The commercial paper can be issued by:

a) All banks b) All corporate

c) All corporate with net worth of at Rs. 1 crore

d) All corporate with net worth of at least Rs. 4 crores

e) Other than those given as options

16. "Ek Bharat Shreshtha Bharat" programme is meant for linking ___ to connect people through

exchanges in areas of language, trade, culture, travel and tourism:

a) States and Cities

b) States and Districts

c) Cities and Towns

d) Districts and Villages

e) None of the above

17. Grameen Bank and Micro Credit are associated with which person?

a) Manmohan Singh

b) Bill Gates

c) Md. Yunus

d) Aung San Su Ki

e) Acharya Vinobha Bhave

18. Many a time we read a term MSS in relation to banking transactions. What is the full form of

MSS?

a) Money Stabilization Scheme

b) Market Stabilization Scheme

c) Maturity and Standardization Service

d) Money Stabilization Service

e) None of the above

19. RBI's open market operation transactions are carried out with a view to regulate?

a) Liquidity in the economy

b) Prices of essential commodities

c) Inflation

d) Only (a) and (c)

e) (a), (b) and (c)

20. What is an Indian Depository Receipt (IDR)?

a) A deposit account with a Public Sector Bank

b) A deposit account with any of depositories in India

c) It is a financial instrument denominated in Indian currency and are issued by a domestic

depository and the underlying equity

d) Shares are secured with a custodian

e) None of the above

21. Which among the following bank/ banks in India have set up the Financial Literacy and

Credit Counseling Centers?

a) Reserve Bank of India

b) Scheduled Commercial Banks

c) Foreign Banks working in India

d) NABARD

e) None of the above

22. Which of the following bank was not nationalized in 1969?

a) Canara Bank

b) United Bank of India

c) UCO Bank

d) Punjab National Bank

e) Andhra Bank

23. Which of the following comes under RBI's quantitative measures?

a) Bank Rate Policy

b) Open Market Operation

c) Cash Reserve Ratio

d) Statutory Liquidity Ratio

e) All the above

24. Prior to the establishment of the Reserve Bank of India, the Government banking business

was conducted by:

a) Bank of India

b) Central Bank of India

c) National Bank of India

d) Imperial Bank of India

e) Punjab National Bank

25. The assets of the banks will be classified as Standard, Substandard,

Doubtful and Loss

assets. Wherein assets which have remained NPA for a period less than or equal to 12 months,

are termed as:

a) Substandard assets

b) Doubtful assets

c) Loss assets

d) Provisional assets

e) Other than those given as

options

26. Govt. has proposed to assist the Startups

through ___ deduction of profits for 3 out of 5

years for startups set up during April 2016 to March 2019.

a) 40%

b) 60%

c) 80%

d) 25%

e) 100%

27. In banking parlance there are certain terms like Demand Deposits and Term Deposits. Term Deposits include:

a) Fixed deposits

b) Recurring deposits

c) Time liabilities portion of saving bank deposits

d) SDR (Short Term Deposits)

e) All of the above

28. Which of the following is not associated with risks related to risk management in banks?

a) Credit risk

b) Market risk

c) Profit risk

d) Operational risk

e) None of these

29. Which of the following is not an authorized mode in Banks to Transfer Money, Know the balance, in the account, etc.?

a) Online

b) Mobile

c) Phone

d) Video Conferencing

e) None of the above

30. A trust is a legal entity authenticated by a:

a) Title deed

b) Sale deed

c) Trust deed

d) Partnership deed

e) Power of attorney

31. Banks allow some important customers to withdraw without clear credit balance. Such facility is known as:

a) Zero Balance

b) Current Account

c) Overdraft

d) Demand draft

e) Promissory

32. To open a savings account in the name of a minor, we should ensure:

a) The person can independently read, write and sign

b) Only operated by self; either physical visits or through ATMs

c) An undertaking furnished by the major guardian

d) Only (a)

e) (a), (b) and (c)

33. Certificate of incorporation of a company is like a:

a) License

b) Permit

c) Clearance

d) Birth certificate

e) Statutory approval

34. To open the account of a public charitable trust, the key document required is:

a) Permission of Charity Commissioner

b) Permission of Local Authority

c) Permission of Court of Law

d) All of the above

e) None of the above

Answers part C

1) e 2) d 3) a 4) e 5) d 6) c 7) b 8) b 9) e 10) a

11) e 12) e 13) b 14) b 15) d 16) b 17) c 18) b 19) e 20) c

21) b 22) e 23) e 24) d 25) a 26) d 27) e 28) c 29) d 30) c

31) c 32) e 33) d 34) a

Questions Part D

1. New Governor of RBI is ....

1) N.Viswanathan

2) Rakesh Mohan

3) Arundhathi Bhattacharya

4) Urjith Patel

5) Subhir Gokarn

2. On 25 August 2016 UPI launched by RBI which revolutionize peer to peer payments in the country, a step closer towards becoming a cashless economy. UPI stands for......

1) United Payments Interface

2) Unified Pay Interface

3) Unique Payments Interface

4) Union Payments Interface

5) Unified Payments Interface

3. Which of the following statements is wrong related to Unified Payments Interface (UPI)?

1) Currently in order to make payments in online, account number, account type, Bank name and IFSC code etc must be entered.

2) But once UPI introduced, interface allow account holders across banks to send and receive money from their smart phones using just their Aadhaar number, mobile number or virtual payments address without entering bank account details.

3) This facility not available to private banks.

4) To initiate a transaction one can use two types of address global

or local. The bank provides

Virtual address similar to email

ID.

5) Virtual address will allow, sending and receiving money from multiple banks and prepaid payment issuers is possible.

4. The RBI has allowed only banks to become Payment Service Providers of UPI service and the Mobile wallets are worrying that their prominence may go away. In this context, which of the following is example for Mobile wallet?

1) Paytm

2) Freecharge

3) Mobikwik

4) Oxigen

5) All of above are the Mobile wallets

5. PhonePe, a Flipkart Group company and which bank launched UPIbased

payment APP?

1) Yes Bank

2) ICICI Bank

3) Andhra Bank

4) Bank of India

5) Bank of Baroda

6. The benefit of UPI (Unified Payments Interface) system of transfer of money is....

1) immediate money transfer through mobile device round the clock 24 X 7 and 365 days.

2) single mobile application for accessing different bank accounts.

3) scheduling PUSH and PULL Payments for various purposes.

4) barcode (Scan and Pay) based payments

5) All of above are the unique benefits of UPI.

7. Which of the following statement is correct relating to the benefit for the banks, once UPI

introduced?

1) Universal Application for transaction

2) Payment basis Single/ Unique Identifier

3) Possibility of seamless merchant transactions

4) Single click two factor authentication

5) All of above

8. Which of the following statement is correct relating to the benefit for the Merchants, once UPI

introduced?

1) Suitable for eCom

& mCom

transaction

2) Tap customers not having credit/ debit

3) Seamless fund collection from customers single

identifiers

4) No risk of storing customer's virtual address like in Cards

5) All of above

9. Which of the following statement is correct relating to the benefit for the Merchants, once UPI

(Unified Payments Interface) introduced?

1) Use of Virtual ID is more secure, no credential sharing

2) Single click authentication

3) Single Application for accessing different bank accounts

4) Raise complaint from Mobile App directly

5) All of above

10. The UPI supports which of the following transactions/ Services ?

1) It can do Pay Request. It means initiating customer is pushing funds to the intended

beneficiary.

2) Collect Request is possible. It is a transaction where the customer is pulling funds from the

intended remitter by using Virtual ID.

3) Generating OTP (One Time Password)

4) Generate/ change PIN

5) All of above transactions/ services available in UPI

11. Till now IMPS (Immediate Payment Service) is the faster mode of transfer of money. What is the additional benefit of UPI (Unified Payments Interface)?

1) Single click two factor authentication

2) Provides for a P2P Pull functionality

3) Single APP for money transfer

4) Simplifies Merchant Payments

5) All of above are the additional benefits of UPI

12. What is the present upper limit of fund transfer using UPI?

1) Rs.10,000

2) Rs.50,000

3) Rs.1 Lakh

4) Rs.2 Lakh

5) Rs.10 Lakh

13. The details of UPI given. Locate the wrong statement.

1) Bank customer needs to register with his/ her PSP (Payment Services Provider) before remitting funds using UPI and link his accounts.

2) Registration of Beneficiary is not required for transferring funds through UPI as the fund would be transferred on the basis of Virtual ID/ Account number and IFSC.

3) Customer cannot link a wallet to UPI, only bank accounts can be added.

4) One customer can use more than one UPI application on the same mobile and link both same as well as different accounts.

5) All of above correct statements

14. RBI constituted the Board for Payment and Settlement Systems in ....

1) 2008

2) 2007

3) 2005

4) 2011

5) 2012

15. NPCI initiated Unified Payments Interface. NPCI stands for ......

1) National Pay Corporation of India

2) National Payments Company of India

3) National Payments Corporation of Initiation

4) National Payments Corporation of India

5) Nodal Payments Corporation of India

16. NPCI is an umbrella organization for all retail payments system in India. It was incorporated

in ......

1) 2010

2) 2011

3) 2009

4) 2008

5) 2013

17. National Payments Corporation of India (NPCI) headed by ....

1) Raghuram Rajan

2) Arundhathi Bhattacharya

3) K.R. Kamath

4) M.Balachandran

5) Urjith Patel

18. To take the banking services to every common man across the country, NPCI (National

Payments Corporation of India) launched *99# service. The *99# service worked on USSD

channel. In this context, USSD stands for ....

1) Unity Supplementary Service Data

2) Unstructured Support Service Data

3) Unstructured Single Service Data

4) Unstructured Supplementary Simple Data

5) Unstructured Supplementary Service Data

19. *99# service introduced in the mobile phones for the inclusion of under banked society. It

was launched by Narendra Modi on 28th August 2014 as part of Pradhan Mantri Jan Dhan

Yojana (PMJDY). Which service available under this service?

1) Check the balance

2) Fund transfer

3) Mini statement request

4) All of above services available

5) None of above service available

at Thursday, September 22, 2016 1 comment

20. *99*99# is a USSD based value added service from NPCI that facilitates the customers

....

1) to know the Rupee and Dollar reference rate.

2) to check the balance in their bank account at the end of last month.

3) to check the credit of TDS in his bank account after 30 September in every year.

4) to check the status of his/ her Aadhaar number seeding/ linking in the bank account.

5) to know whether the OD was granted under JDY account.

21. On 25 August 2016, RBI issued a notification regarding the loans to women Self Help

Groups. Pick up wrong statement.

1) SHGs will be eligible for interest subvention on credit up to Rs.3 lakh.

2) The rate of Interest is at 7% per annum under Deendayal Antyodaya YojanaNational

Rural

Livelihood Mission.

3) However SHGs availing capital subsidy under Swarnajayanti Gram Swarozgar Yojana

(SGSY) in their existing credit outstanding will not be eligible for benefit under this scheme.

4) The banks lend to a women SHGs in 250 districts as per this notification.

5) All of above statements correct

22. Chillr and Federal Bank joined hands for cashless transactions. Chillr is a ....

1) Small Finance Bank

2) New Payment rank

3) Mobile banking application

4) HDFC bank subsidiary Coordinated

mutual fund company

5) Insurance company

23. Which bank launched a payment service using a smart phone keyboard named 'iMobile

SmartKeys' to make mobile payments easier?

1) Andhra Bank

2) SBI

3) ICICI Bank

4) HDFC

5) Union Bank of India

24. Jawaharlal Nehru Port Trust in Navi Mumbai signed an agreement with SBI and

Development Bank of Singapore for ECB to the tune $400 Million. In this context, the term ECB

stands for .....

1) Exit Commercial Borrowing

2) Elective commercial Borrowing

3) External Commercial Board

4) Economical Commercial Borrowing

5) External Commercial Borrowing

25. 11th G 20

summit concluded at....

1) Hangzhou of China

2) Tokyo of Japan

3) New Delhi of India

4) Rome of Italy

5) Ottawa of Canada

Answers part D:

14,

25,

33,

45,

51,

65,

75,

85,

95,

105

115,

123,

135,

143,

154,

164,

174,

185,

194,

204,

215,

223,

233,

245,

251

Questions part E

1. India was ranked 67th at the 2016 Rio Olympics. Which is the other country that was also

ranked 67th?

1) Bulgaria

2) Venezuela

3) Mexico

4) Lithuania

5) Mongolia

2. The 14th edition of Pravasi Bharatiya Divas will be held in January 2017 in?

1) New Delhi

2) Bengalore

3) Jaipur

4) Hyderabad

5) Mumbai

3. The 13th IndiaEuropean

Union Summit was held on March 30, 2016 in?

1) New Delhi

2) Mumbai

3) Brussels

4) London

5) Paris

4. The South Asian Association for Regional Cooperation (SAARC) Disaster Management

Centre

will be established in which of the following countries?

1) Nepal

2) Bangladesh

3) Maldives

4) India

5) Sri Lanka

5. Who was awarded the 2016 Abel Prize for mathematics?

1) Artur Avila

2) Manjul Bhargava

3) Louis Nirenberg

4) John Nash

5) Sir Andrew Wiles

6. Which football team won the 2016 African Nations Championship held in Rwanda?

1) Democratic Republic of Congo

2) Mali

3) Ivory Coast

4) Niger

5) Nigeria

7. Which country will host the 2018

African Nations Championship

football tournament?

1) Ivory Coast

2) Sudan

3) Tunisia

4) South Africa

5) Kenya

8. The 12th South Asian Games in February 2016 were cohosted by?

1) Kolkata and Guwahati

2) Guwahati and Shillong

3) Agartala and Shillong

4) Agartala and Itanagar

5) Kolkata and Agartala

9. The 13th edition of the South Asian Games will be held in 2018 in which of the following countries?

1) Bhutan

2) Bangladesh

3) Nepal

4) Sri Lanka

5) Maldives

10. LAMITYE 2016 is a joint military training exercise between Indian Army and the Army of:

1) Maldives

2) France

3) Sri Lanka

4) Seychelles

5) Japan

11. Swami Vivekananda International Airport is located in?

1) Ranchi, Jharkhand

2) Cuttack, Odisha

3) Rajkot, Gujarat

4) Ratnagiri, Maharashtra

5) Raipur, Chhattisgarh

12. The Banks Board Bureau (BBB) will select the heads of:

1) Regional Rural Banks

2) Public Sector Banks

3) Private Sector Banks

4) Payments Banks

5) Small Finance Banks

13. The "Kishore" scheme under the Pradhan Mantri MUDRA Yojana (PMMY) offers maximum loan of:

1) Rs. 50,000

2) Rs. 2 lakh

3) Rs. 5 lakh

4) Rs 10. lakh

5) None of these

14. Indradhanush is a seven pronged plan to revamp:

1) Cooperative Banks

2) Microfinance Institutions

3) Private Sector Banks

4) Public Sector Banks

5) None of these

15. Which of the following Central Universities celebrated its 100th year in 2016?

1) University of Allahabad

2) Aligarh Muslim University

3) Visva Bharati University

4) University of Delhi

5) Banaras Hindu University

16. Safra Catz visited India recently. She is the Chief Executive Officer of:

1) IBM

2) Intel

3) Oracle

4) Yahoo

5) Facebook

17. Indian Institute of Millets Research (IIMR) is a premier agricultural research institute located in:

1) Hyderabad

2) Cuttack

3) Bangalore

4) Chennai

5) Nagpur

18. The National Deworming Day is observed by the Ministry of Health and Family Welfare on:

1) March 5

2) March 10

3) February 5

4) January 25

5) February 10

19. Which of the following books is NOT written by Pranab Mukherjee?

1) The Turbulent Years: 19801996

2) The Dramatic Decade: The Indira Gandhi Years

3) Thoughts and Reflections

4) Beyond Survival: Emerging Dimensions of Indian Economy

5) The Unseen Indira Gandhi

20. India participated for the first time in the Cobra Gold multilateral amphibious exercise hosted by:

1) China

2) Thailand

3) Pakistan

4) Philippines

5) Japan

21. "Setu Bharatam" is a central government program that aims at making all National Highways railway level crossing free by the year:

1) 2019

2) 2020

3) 2021

4) 2022

5) 2025

22. The Mesabi Iron Range is the chief iron ore mining district in:

1) Brazil

2) USA

3) Australia

4) South Africa

5) Kenya

23. Who became the first civilian President of Myanmar after over 50 years of military rule on March 30, 2016?

1) Myint Swe

2) Henry Van Thio

3) Htin Kyaw

4) Thein Sein

5) None of these

24. Ahmed Aboul Gheit is the present Secretary General of the Arab League. He is former Foreign Minister of:

1) Morocco

2) Qatar

3) Tunisia

4) Egypt

5) Bahrain

25. Dominic Asquith is which country's High Commissioner to India?

1) Canada

2) New Zealand

3) Australia

4) Jamaica

5) UK

26. Tribhuvan International Airport is situated in:

1) Bangkok, Thailand

2) Colombo, Sri Lanka

3) Kathmandu, Nepal

4) Jakarta, Indonesia

5) Putrajaya, Malaysia

27. What is the currency of Mauritius?

1) Mauritius Riel

2) Mauritius Dollar

3) Mauritius Rupee

4) Mauritius Pound

5) None of these

28. Who has been appointed as the Chairperson of the 21st Law Commission?

1) Justice C.K. Prasad

2) Justice Cyriac Joseph

3) Justice N. Santosh Hegde

4) Justice Balbir Singh Chauhan

5) Justice Umesh Chandra Banerjee

29. Who won the 2016 Pritzker Architecture Prize?

1) Wang Shu, China

2) Alejandro Aravena, Chile

3) Peter Zumthor, Switzerland

4) Kazuyo Sejima, Japan

5) None of these

30. Global Risks Report is an annual study published by the:

1) World Bank

2) International Monetary Fund

3) World Economic Forum

4) World Trade Organization

5) None of these

31. Who was appointed as the Chairman of Central Administrative Tribunal in March 2016?

1) Justice Permod Kohli

2) Justice Arun Tandon

3) Justice A.K. Mittal

4) Justice Ajay Tewari

5) Justice Jaswant Singh

32. "The High Mountains of Portugal" is a 2016 novel written by:

1) David Mitchell

2) Yann Martel

3) Graham Swift

4) Jerry Pinto

5) None of these

33. Lloyd S. Shapley of USA passed away on March 12, 2016. He won the 2012 Nobel Prize in:

1) Physics

2) Chemistry

3) Economics

4) Medicine

5) Literature

34. Who has been appointed the first Chairman of the Banks Board Bureau?

1) H.N. Sinor

2) R. Gandhi

3) Anil Kahandelwal

4) Vinod Rai

5) None of these

35. Andrew Holness is the present Prime Minister of:

1) Antigua

2) Barbados

3) Dominica

4) Saint Lucia

5) Jamaica

36. In March 2016, Barack Obama became the first US President in 88 years to visit which of the following countries?

1) Japan

2) Argentina

3) North Korea

4) Cuba

5) Libya

37. Which country topped the World Happiness Index, according to the World Happiness Report 2016?

1) Denmark

2) Canada

3) Iceland

4) Switzerland

5) Norway

38. What is India's rank in the World Happiness Index 2016?

1) 117

2) 118

3) 116

4) 121

5) 130

39. Martin Crowe died on March 3, 2016 at the age of 53. He was the greatest batsman of?

1) West Indies

2) Australia

3) New Zealand

4) South Africa

5) None of these

40. The 4th World Congress of Biosphere Reserves was held in March 2016 in:

1) Chile, Santiago

2) Ankara, Turkey

3) Brisbane, Australia

4) Lima, Peru

5) Jakarta, Indonesia

ANSWERS part E
1) 5 2) 2 3) 3 4) 4 5) 5 6) 1 7) 5 8) 2 9) 3 10) 4

11) 5 12) 2 13) 3 14) 4 15) 5 16) 3 17) 1 18) 5 19) 5 20) 2

21) 1 22) 2 23) 3 24) 4 25) 5 26) 3 27) 3 28) 4 29) 2 30) 3

31) 1 32) 2 33) 3 34) 4 35) 5 36) 4 37) 1 38) 2 39) 3 40) 4

Questions part F
1. Who has been appointed as new Chairman of Central Silkboard?

A) Anil Agarwal

B) Anand Mahindra

C) Achyuts Samanta

D) K.M. Hanumantarayappa

E) Rangarajan

2. Who was appointed as Managing Director of State Bank of India?

A) Dinesh Kumar Khara

B) Sandeep Kumar Khara

C) Dilip Sagvi

D) Ashok Soota

E) Laxmi Mittal

3. Who has been selected for the 23rd Rajiv Gandhi National Sadbhavana Award 2016?

A) Singer Shubha Mudgal

B) C. Ajit Kumar

C) R Naveen

D) L. Samayasri

E) Priyarshini

4. The 2016 Kabaddi World Cup will be hosted by which country?

A) Nepal

B) Bhutan

C) Bangladesh

D) Pakistan

E) India

5. Which has announced a 0.05% reduction in its Marginal Cost of funds based Lending Rate

(MCLR)?

A) Axis Bank

B) RBI

C) ICICI Bank

D) SBI

E) HSBC

6. World Bank has approved a .... credit from the International Development Association

(IDA) to support the Sri Lanka's economic reforms programme.

A) $10 million

B) $50 million

C) $100 million

D) $120 million

E) $80 million

7. .... Bank tied up with a fintech startup

Fisdom for personal wealth management services.

A) Axis Bank

B) RBI

C) ICICI Bank

D) SBI

E) BOB

8. The main aim of SBI's certification program for officers who sanction loans to ...

A) Reduce NPA'S

B) Reach targets

C) Upgrade them

D) Increase the standards

E) None of these

9. 'Grassroots Innovation' book written by ......

A) Prof. Anil K. Gupta

B) Amitav Ghosh

C) Shashi Tharoor

D) Aravind Adiga

E) Vikram Seth

10. Nobel Laureate Ahmed Zewail has passed away recently. He belongs to which country?

A) Egypt

B) Spain

C) USA

D) China

E) India

11. Which payments company recently announced the partnership with IRCTC's food app?

A) Mobikwik

B) Paytm

C) Freecharge

D) Post payment

E) Quicker

12. ICICI Bank ties up with Apollo India Credit Opportunity Management LLC and AION Capital Management to form ....

A) Bank Accurance

B) Payment Bank

C) Joint Venture

D) NBFI

E) Asset Reconstruction Company

13. CBI has been made the nodal authority for banks to report high value frauds worth over .... in public sector banks.

A) Rs.80 crore

B) Rs.50 crore

C) Rs.100 crore

D) Rs.55 crore

E) Rs.60 crore

14. IBM in partnership with .... launched a global development hub called Garage for iOS apps

in Bengaluru.

A) APPLE

B) SAMSUNG

C) XIOMI

D) HTC

E) MICROMAX

15. Name the typhoon made its landfall near Dapeng Peninsula in China's Guangdong province?

A) Nida

B) Rina

C) Gert

D) Otto

E) Julia

16. German Engineering major Siemens Ltd. has received an order worth approximately Rs.217 crore for power project in which of the following country?

A) Pakistan

B) Myanmar

C) Nepal

D) Bangladesh

E) India

17. Which one of the following countries Cabinet approved a fresh economic stimulus package of worth more than $275 billions?

A) Canada

B) France

C) Norway

D) China

E) Japan

18. Which of the following country has assured India support for UNSC high seat?

A) Philippines

B) Vietnam

C) Malaysia

D) Indonesia

E) Thailand

19. Which state government has decided to recruit members of transgender community as

warders in jails of the State?

A) Bihar

B) Kerala

C) Odisha

D) Maharashtra

E) Punjab

20. Central body approves .... crore rupees for Ganga rejuvenation projects.

A) Rs.400 crore

B) Rs.425 crore

C) Rs.450 crore

D) Rs.475 crore

E) Rs.500 crore

21. Railway Minister Suresh Prabhu recently lays foundation stone of broadgage

rail project in

which state?

A) Mizoram

B) Nagaland

C) Haryana

D) Tripura

E) Meghalaya

22. Resolution for renaming of which high court passed recently by the state assembly?

A) Mumbai High Court

B) Kolkata High Court

C) Delhi High Court

D) Kerala High Court

E) Madras High Court

23. How many Jan Aushadhi Stores to be opened across India under Pradhan Mantri Jan

Aushadhi Yojana?

A) 1500

B) 2500

C) 3500

D) 4500

E) 3000

24. Former Comptroller and Auditor General (CAG) of India Vinod Rai has stepped down from

which private sector lender?

A) AXIS

B) HDFC

C) ICICI

D) YES

E) IDFC

25. Yuriko Koike elected as .... first female governor.

A) Moscow

B) Tokyo

C) Beijing

D) Shangai

E) None

26. Which state become the first state to approve sewage & waste water policy?

A) Nagaland

B) Rajasthan

C) Andhrapradesh

D) Gujarath

E) Odisa

27. Amazon launches fulfilment centre for prime deliveries in which city of india?

A) Pune

B) New Delhi

C) Bangalore

D) Chennai

E) Mumbai

28. Which university to perform world's CRISPRCas9

first genetic editing trial on humans

aiming to cure lung cancer?

A) Sichuan University

B) Stanford University

C) Harvard University

D) University of Cambridge

E) University of Bristol

29. Which program is launched by the Minister of Communications Manoj Sinha for Telecom and

Postal Service users can now file complaints with the government directly?

A) Twitter Sewa

B) Facebook Sewa

C) Twitter Jana

D) Facebook Jana

E) None

30. Which country has successfully launched its first mobile telecom satellite "Tiantong01"?

A) France

B) China

C) South Korea

D) Japan

E) Germany

31. Centre to organise 'Make in India' conference in which of the following city?

A) Bhubaneswar

B) Mumbai

C) Thiruvanthapuram

D) Bangalore

E) Nagpur

32. SAARC Immigration Authorities meeting held in which of the following city?

A) New Delhi

B) Islamabad

C) Kathmandu

D) Kabul

E) Dhaka

33. The National Handloom Day is celebrated on which day in India?

A) August 7

B) August 8

C) August 5

D) August 6

E) August 11

34. Who won the STAR SportsProKabaddi

League 2016?

A) Patna Pirates

B) Telugu Titans

C) Jaipur Pink Panthers

D) Dabang Delhi

E) Bangalore Bulls

35. Vishu a Hindu festival celebrated in which of the following states?

A) Andhra Pradesh

B) Telangana

C) Kerala

D) Assam

E) Manipur

Answers Part E

1D,

2A,

3A,

4E,

5C,

6C,

7E,

8A,

9A,

10A

11A,

12E,

13B,

14A,

15A,

16D,

17E,

18B,

19C,

20A

21B,

22E,

23E,

24E,

25B,

26B,

27D,

28A,

29A,

30B

31A,

32B,

33A,

34A,

35C

Questions part F

1. Justice Iqbal Ahmed Ansari sworn in as Chief Justice of .... High Court.

A) Jaipur

B) Guwahati

C) Mumbai

D) Bhopal

E) Patna

2. Theresa May appointed Prime Minister of which of the following country?

A) France

B) Germany

C) Poland

D) United Kingdom

E) Brazil

3. Who won Ramon Magsaysay award for 2016?

A) T.M. Krishna

B) Bezwada Wilson

C) Arvind Kejriwal

D) Both A and B

E) None

4. Which states tourism won the gold at Pacific Asia Travel Association (PATA) awards?

A) Gujarat

B) Maharashtra

C) Kerala

D) Tamilnadu

E) Telangana

5. What is the maximum value of soiled currency notes which can be exchanged for free of

charge?

A) 5000

B) 25000

C) 2000

D) 1000

E) None

6. Which of the following banks have become first Indian banks to join SWIFT's global

payments innovation initiative?

A) ICICI Bank and Axis Bank

B) ICICI Bank and SBI

C) HDFC Bank and UCO Bank

D) SBI and Indian Bank

E) SBI and BOB

7. Who among the following will lead the Interregulatory Working Group on Fin Tech and Digital Banking?

A) N. Srinivasan

B) Sai Kumar

C) Sudarshan Sen

D) N.V. Swami

E) Bobby Jindal

8. Indian Railways has recently signed MoU with which of the following banks to promote rail ticketing?

A) ICICI Bank

B) UCO Bank

C) SBI Bank

D) Yes Bank

E) Axis Bank

9. "Who Moved My Interest Rate?" written by...

A) Ruskin Bond

B) Nayantara Sahgal

C) C. D. Deshmukh

D) Duvvuri Subbarao

E) Manmohan Singh

10. Amal Dutta has passed away recently he belongs to which of the following sport?

A) Cricket

B) Hockey

C) Football

D) Chess

E) Golf

11. India has approved a $ 318 million loan for which country railways?

A) Nepal

B) Sri Lanka

C) Afghanistan

D) Myanmar

E) None

12. Myntra acquired which ecommerce

portal?

A) Flipkart

B) Lifestyle

C) ebay

D) Just buy

E) Jabong

13. emarketplace

web portal has been launched by which union ministry for goods

procurement?

A) Ministry of Micro, Small and Medium Enterprises

B) Ministry of Environment, Forest and Climate Change

C) Ministry of Commerce and Industry

D) Ministry of Communications and Information Technology

E) None of these

14. Which of the following Indian Bank have been listed in the 2016 Fortune 500 list of the

world's biggest corporations in terms of revenue?

A) SBI Bank

B) ICICI Bank

C) UCO Bank

D) Yes Bank

E) Axis Bank

15. Which of the following country has declared threemonth

state of emergency after a failed

military coup to overthrow the democratically elected government?

A) Singapore

B) Turkey

C) Nepal

D) Qatar

E) Mexico

16. Madeira international airport to be named after?

A) Radamel Falcao

B) Lionel Messi

C) Cristiano Ronaldo

D) Andres Iniesta

E) Sergio Ramos

17. Fedor Konyukhov, has broken the record for the fastest circumnavigation of the Earth in a

hot air balloon in just over 11 days. He belongs which of the following country?

A) Cuba

B) Russia

C) Cyprus

D) Brunei

E) Bahrain

18. Government to set up committee to tackle shortage of pulses headed by ....

A) Narendra Modi

B) Arun Jaitley

C) Rajnath Singh

D) Harsh Vardhan

E) Prakash Javadekar

19. Union Cabinet approves disinvestment of .... percent in National Buildings

Construction Corporation Limited (NBCC).

A) 10%

B) 15%

C) 20%

D) 25%

E) 12.5%

20. India and Nepal launched bus service between two connecting which of the following

famous cities?

A) New Delhi and Kathmandu

B) New Delhi and Birgunj

C) New Delhi and Biratnagar

D) New Delhi and Patan

E) New Delhi and Pokhara

21. Railways launch timetabled

Auto Express between which of the following cities?

A) Gurgaon to Nidvanda

B) Mumbai to New Delhi

C) Mumbai to Ahmedabad

D) Gurgaon to Mumbai

E) Ahmedabad to New Delhi

22. India's first green train corridor opens in ....

A) Andhra Pradesh

B) Maharashtra

C) Gujarat

D) Tamilnadu

E) Kerala

23. Who among the following named brand ambassador of the Craig McDermott International Cricket Academy in Australia?

A) Virat Kohli

B) MS Dhoni

C) Suresh Raina

D) Rohit Sharma

E) Shikar Dhawan

24. Who among the following is the highestpaid banker in India?

A) Chanda Kochhar

B) Aditya Puri

C) Shika Sharma

D) Sudarshan Sen

E) None

25. National Banana Research Centre to be set up in which state?

A) Tamilnadu

B) Kerala

C) Maharashtra

D) Karnataka

E) Bihar

26. India's first smart grid to setup in which of the following state?

A) Haryana

B) Gujarat

C) Rajasthan

D) Bihar

E) Sikkim

27. Microsoft introduced a new program aimed at growing Surface's footprint in the business
called as ....

A) Surface of motion

B) Surface as a platform

C) Surface as a service

D) Surface as a support

E) None

28. NASA is planned to give final design and construction of its next Mars Rover to be launched
by which year?

A) 2019

B) 2020

C) 2017

D) 2018

E) 2022

29. Which country to conduct world's first Zika vaccine test on humans?

A) Thailand

B) Canada

C) France

D) China

E) South Korea

30. 9th edition of Indian Fashion Jewellery & Accessories Show to begin in which of the
following city?

A) New Delhi

B) Mumbai

C) Bangalore

D) Hyderabad

E) Kolkata

31. A threeday

meeting between Border Security Force (BSF) and Border Guard Bangladesh

(BGB) has begun in......

A) Patna

B) Dispur

C) Hyderabad

D) Agartala

E) None

32. International Nelson Mandela Day is observed on which date?

A) July 28

B) July 17

C) July 18

D) July 15

E) July 22

33. Who won men's singles title of 2016 Wimbledon?

A) Andy Murrey

B) Rafael Nadal

C) Roger Federer

D) Novak Djokovic

E) Stan Wawrinka

34. World AntiDoping

Agency (WADA) called which of the following country to be completely

banned from the Rio Olympics and other international sport?

A) Russia

B) China

C) US

D) India

E) Srilanka

35. Which state to geotag

irrigation projects with the help of NRSA, Icrisat?

A) Andhra Pradesh

B) Telangana

C) Tamilnadu

D) Kerala

E) Karnataka

Answers part F

1E,

2D

, 3D,

4C,

5A,

6A,

7C,

8C,

9D,

10C

11B,

12E,

13C,

14A,

15B,

16C,

17B,

18B,

19B,

20E

21A,

22D,

23B,

24B,

25E,

26A,

27C,

28B,

29B,

30A

31D,

32C,

33A,

34A,

35B

Questions and Answers part G

1. With reference to 'stand up india scheme', which of the following statement

is/are correct?

1. Its purpose is to promote entrepreneurship among SC/ST and women entrepreneurs.

2. It provides for refinance through SIDBI.

Select the correct answer using the code given below.

(a) 1 only

(b) 2 only

(c) Both 1 and 2

(d) Neither 1 nor 2

Answer . c

2. The FAO accords the status of 'Globally Important Agricultural Heritage System (GIAHS)' to traditional agricultural systems. What is the overall goal of this initiative?

1. To provide modern technology, training in modern farming methods and financial support to local communities of identified GIAHS so as to greatly enhance their agricultural productivity

2. To identify and safeguard ecofriendly traditional farm practices and their associated landscapers, agricultural biodiversity and knowledge systems of the local communities

3. To provide Geographical Indication status to all the varieties of agricultural produce in such identified GIAHS

Select the correct answer using the code given below.

(a) 1 and 3 only

(b) 2 only

(C) 2 and 3 only

(d) 1, 2 and 3

Answer. b

3. Which of the following is/are tributary tributaries of Brahmaputra?

1. Dibang

2. Kameng

3. Lohit

Select the correct answer using the code given below.

(a) 1 only

(b) 2 and 3 only

(c) 1 and 3 only

(d) 1, 2 and 3

Answer.d

4. The term 'Core Banking Solutions' is sometimes seen in the news. Which of the following statements best describes/describe this term?

1. It is a networking of a bank's branches which enables customers to operate their accounts from any branch of the bank on its network regardless of where they open their accounts.

2. It is an effort to increase RBI's control over commercial banks through computerization.

3. It is a detailed procedure by which a bank with huge nonperforming

assets is taken

over by another bank.

Select the correct answer using the code given below.

(a) 1 only

(b) 2 and 3 only

(c) 1 and 3 only

(d) 1, 2 and 3

Answer . a

5. Consider the following pairs :

Terms sometimes Their origin

seen in the news

1. Annex—I Countries : Cartagena Protocol

2. Certified Emissions Reductions : Nagoya Protocol

3. Clean Development Mechanism : Kyoto Protocol

71

Which of the pairs given above is/are correctly matched?

(a) 1 and 2 only

(b) 2 and 3 only

(c) 3 only

(d) 1, 2 and 3

Answer . c

6. In the context of the developments in Bioinformatics, the term transcriptome',

sometimes seen in the news, refers to

(a) a range of enzymes used in genome editing

(b) the full range of mRNA molecules expressed by an organism

(c) the description of the mechanism of gene expression

(d) a mechanism of genetic mutations taking place in cells

Answer . b

7. 'Mission Indradhanush' launched by the Government of India pertains to

(a) immunization of children and pregnant women

(b) construction of smart cities across the country

(c) India's own search for the Earthlike

planets in outer space

(d) New Educational Policy

Answer . a

8. Which of the following best describes/ describe the aim of 'Green India

Mission' of the Government of India?

1. Incorporating environment al benefits and costs into the Union and State Budgets

thereby implementing the `green accounting'

2. Launching the second green revolution to enhance agricultural output so as to ensure

food security to one and all in the future

3. Restoring and enhancing forest cover and responding to climate change by a

combination of adaptation and mitigation measures

Select the correct answer using the code given below.

(a) 1 only

(b) 2 and 3 only

(c) 3 only

(d) 1, 2 and 3

Answer . c

9. With reference to prepackaged

items in India, it is mandatoy to the

manufacturer to put which of the following information on the main label, as per

the Food Safety and Standards (Packaging and Labelling) Regulations, 2011?

1. List of ingredients including additives

2. Nutrition information

3. Recommendations, if any, made by the medical profession about the possibility of any

allergic reactions

4. Vegetarian/nonvegetarian

Select the correct answer using the code given below.

(a) 1, 2 and 3

(b) 2, 3 and 4

(c) 1, 2 and 4

(d) 1 and 4 only

Answer . c

10. 'Project Loon', sometimes seen in the news, is related to

(a) waste management technology

(b) wireless communication technology

(c) solar power production technology

(d) water conservation technology

Answer . b

11. 'Net metering' is sometimes seen in the news in the context of promoting the

(a) production and use of solar energy by the households/consumers

(b) use of piped natural gas in the kitchens of households

(c) installation of CNG kits in motorcars

(d) installation of water meters in urban households

Answer . a

12. India's ranking in the 'Ease of Doing Business Index' is sometimes seen in the

news. Which of the following has declared that ranking?

(a) Organization for Economic Cooperation and Development (OECD)

(b) World Economic Forum

(c) World Bank

(d) World Trade Organization (WTO)

Answer . c

13. Banjaras during the medieval period of Indian history were generally

(a) agriculturists

(b) warriors

(c) weavers

(d) traders

Answer . d

14. Who of the following had first deciphered the edicts of Emperor Ashoka?

(a) Georg Bilhler

(b) James Prinsep

(c) Max Muller

(d) William Jones

Answer . b

15. With reference to the 'Gram Nyayalaya Act', which of the following statements

is/are correct?

1. As per the Act, Gram Nyayalayas can hear only civil cases and not criminal cases.

2. The Act allows local social activists as mediators/reconciliators.

Select the correct answer using the code given below.

(a) 1 only

(b) 2 only

(c) Both 1 and 2

(d) Neither 1 nor 2

Answer . b

16. With reference to the 'TransPacific

Partnership', consider the following

statements :

1. It is an agreement among all the Pacific Rim countries except China and Russia.

2. It is a strategic alliance for the purpose of maritime security only.

Which of the statements given above is/are correct?

(a) 1 only

(b) 2 only

(c) Both 1 and 2

(d) Neither 1 nor 2

Answer . a

17. Consider the following statements :

The IndiaAfrica

Summit

1. held in 2015 was the third such Summit

2. was actually initiated by Jawaharlal Nehru in 1951

Which of the statements given above is/are correct?

(a) 1 only

(b) 2 only

(c) Both 1 and 2

(d) Neither 1 nor 2

Answer . a

18. What is/are the purpose/purposes of the `Marginal Cost of Funds based

Lending Rate (MCLR)' announced by RBI?

1. These guidelines help improve the transparency in the methodology followed by

banks for determining the interest rates on advances.

2. These guidelines help ensure availability of bank credit at interest rates which are fair

to the borrowers as well as the banks.

Select the correct answer using the code given below.

(a) 1 only

(b) 2 only

(c) Both 1 and 2

(d) Neither 1 nor 2

Answer .c

19. What is/are unique about 'Kharai camel', a breed found in India?

1. It is capable of swimming up to three kilometres in seawater.

2. It survives by grazing on mangroves.

3. It lives in the wild and cannot be domesticated.

Select the correct answer using the code given below.

(a) 1 and 2 only

(b) 3 only

(c) 1 and 3 only (d) 1, 2 and 3

Answer . d

20. Recently, our scientists have discovered a new and distinct species of

banana plant which attains a height of about 11 metres and has orangecoloured fruit pulp. In which part of India has it been discovered?

(a) Andaman Islands

(b) Anaimalai Forests

(c) Maikala Hills

(d) Tropical rain forests of northeast

Answer .a

21. Which one of the following is the best description of 'INS Astradharini', that

was in the news recently?

(a) Amphibious warfare ship

(b) Nuclearpowered

submarine

(c) Torpedo launch and recovery vessel

(d) Nuclearpowered

aircraft carrier

Answer . c

22. What is 'Greased Lightning10

(GL10)',

recently in the news?

(a) Electric plane tested by NASA

(b) Solarpowered

twoseater

aircraft designed by Japan

(c) Space observatory launched by China

(d) Reusable rocket designed by ISRO

Answer . a

23. With reference to 'Initiative for Nutritional Security through Intensive Millets

Promotion', which of the following statements is/are correct?

1. This initiative aims to demonstrate the improved production and postharvest technologies, and to demonstrate value addition techniques, in an integrated manner, with cluster approach.

2. Poor, small, marginal and tribal farmers have larger stake in this scheme.

3. An important objective of the scheme is to encourage farmers of commercial crops to shift to millet cultivation by offering them free kits of critical inputs of nutrients and microirrigation equipment.

Select the correct answer using the code given below.

(a) 1 only

(b) 2 and 3 only

(c) 1 and 2 only

(d) 1, 2 and 3

Answer . a

24. The `Swadeshi' and 'Boycott' were adopted as methods of struggle for the

first time during the

(a) agitation against the Partition of Bengal

(b) Home Rule Movement

(c) NonCooperation

Movement

(d) visit of the Simon Commission to India

Answer . a

25. With reference to the religious history of India, consider the following

statements :

1. The concept of Bodhisattva is central to Hinayana sect of Buddhism.

2. Bodhisattva is a compassionate one on his way to enlightenment.

3. Bodhisattva delays achieving his own salvation to help all sentient beings on their path

to it.

Which of the statements given above is/are correct?

(a) 1 only

(b) 2 and 3 only

(c) 2 only

(d) 1, 2 and 3

Answer . b

26. 'Doctors Without Borders (Medecins Sans Frontieres)', often in the news, is

(a) a division of World Health Organization

(b) a nongovernmental

international organization

(c) an intergovernmental

agency sponsored by European Union

(d) a specialized agency of the United Nations

Answer . b

27. With reference to an initiative called 'The Economics of Ecosystems and

Biodiversity (TEEB)', which of the following statements is/are correct?

1. It is an initiative hosted by UNEP, IMF and World Economic Forum.

2. It is a global initiative that focuses on drawing attention to the economic benefits of

biodiversity.

3. It presents an approach that can help decisionmakers

recognize, demonstrate and

capture the value of ecosystems and biodiversity.

Select the correct answer using the code given below.

(a) 1 and 2 only

(b) 3 only

(c) 2 and 3 only

(d) 1, 2 and 3

Answer . c

28. With reference to 'Red Sanders', sometimes seen in the news, consider the

following statements:

1. It is a tree species found in a part of South India.

2. It is one of the most important trees in the tropical rain forest areas of South India.

Which of the statements given above is/are correct?

(a) 1 only

(b) 2 only

(c) Both 1 and 2

(d) Neither 1 nor 2

Answer .c

29. Which of the following statements is/are correct?

Proper design and effective implementation of UNREDD+

Programme can

significantly contribute to

1. protection of biodiversity

2. resilience of forest ecosystems

3. poverty reduction

Select the correct answer using the code given below.

(a) 1 and 2 only

(b) 3 only

(c) 2 and 3 only

(d) 1, 2 and 3

Answer . d

30. What is 'Greenhouse Gas Protocol'?

(a) It is an international accounting tool for government and business leaders to

understand, quantify and manage greenhouse gas emissions

(b) It is an initiative of the United Nations to offer financial incentives to developing

countries to reduce greenhouse gas emissions and to adopt ecofriendly

technologies

(c) It is an intergovernmental

agreement ratified by all the member countries of the

United Nations to reduce greenhouse gas emissions to specified levels by the year

2022

(d) It is one of the multilateral REDD+ initiatives hosted by the World Bank

Answer . a

31. With reference to 'Financial Stability and Development Council', consider the

following statements :

1. It is an organ of NITI Aayog.

2. It is headed by the Union Finance Minister.

3. It monitors macroprudential supervision of the economy.

Which of the statements given above is/are correct?

(a) 1 and 2 only

(b) 3 only

(c) 2 and 3 only

(d) 1, 2 and 3

Answer . c

32. With reference to 'Agenda 21', sometimes seen in the news, consider the

following statements :

1. It is a global action plan for sustainable development

2. It originated in the World Summit on Sustainable Development held in Johannesburg

in 2002.

Which of the statements given above is/are correct?

 (a) 1 only

(b) 2 only

(c) Both 1 and 2

(d) Neither 1 nor 2

Answer . a

33. Satya Shodhak Samaj organized

(a) a movement for upliftment of tribals in Bihar

(b) a templeentry

movement in Gujarat

(c) an anticaste

movement in Maharashtra

(d) a peasant movement in Punjab

Answer .c

34. Which of the following statements is/are correct?

Viruses can infect

1. bacteria

2. fungi

3. plants

Select the correct answer using the code given below.

(a) 1 and 2 only

(b) 3 only

(c) 1 and 3 only

(d) 1, 2 and 3

Answer . d

35. The term 'Base Erosion and Profit Shifting' is sometimes seen in the news in

the context of

(a) mining operation by multinational companies in resourcerich

but backward areas

(b) curbing of the tax evasion by multinational companies

(c) exploitation of genetic resources of a country by multinational companies

(d) lack of consideration of environmental costs in the planning and implementation of developmental projects

Answer . b

36. Recently, India's first 'National Investment and Manufacturing Zone' was proposed to be set up in

(a) Andhra Pradesh

(b) Gujarat

(c) Maharashtra

(d) Uttar Pradesh

Answer . a

37. What is/are the purpose/purposes of `District Mineral Foundations' in India?

1. Promoting mineral exploration activities in mineralrich

districts

2. Protecting the interests of the persons affected by mining operations

3. Authorizing State Governments to issue licences for mineral exploration

Select the correct answer using the code given below.

(a) 1 and 2 only

(b) 2 only

(c) 1 and 3 only

(d) 1, 2 and 3

Answer .b

38. `SWAYAM', an initiative of the Government of India, aims at

(a) promoting the Self Help Groups in rural areas

(b) providing financial and technical assistance to young startup

entrepreneurs

(c) promoting the education and health of adolescent girls

(d) providing affordable and quality education to the citizens for free

Answer . d

39. The MontagueChelmsford

Proposals were related to

(a) social reforms

(b) educational reforms

(c) reforms in police administration

(d) constitutional reforms

Answer . d

40. What is/are common to the two historical places known as Ajanta and

Mahabalipuram?

1. Both were built in the same period.

2. Both belong to the same religious denomination.

3. Both have rockcut

monuments.

Select the correct answer using the code given below.

(a) 1 and 2 only

(b) 3 only

(c) 1 and 3 only

(d) None of the statements given above is correct

Answer . c

41. With reference to 'Bitcoins', sometimes seen in the news, which of the

following statements is/are correct?

1. Bitcoins are tracked by the Central Banks of the countries.

2. Anyone with a Bitcoin address can send and receive Bitcoins from anyone else with a

Bitcoin address.

3. Online payments can be sent without either side knowing the identity of the other.

Select the correct answer using the code given below.

(a) 1 and 2 only

(b) 2 and 3 only

(c) 3 only

(d) 1, 2 and 3

Answer . b

42. Consider the following statements :

1. New Development Bank has been set up by APEC.

2. The headquarters of New Development Bank is in Shanghai.

Which of the statements given above is/are correct?

(a) 1 only

(b) 2 only

(c) Both 1 and 2

(d) Neither 1 nor 2

Answer . b

43. 'Gadgil Committee Report' and 'Kasturirangan Committee Report', sometimes

seen in the news, are related to

(a) constitutional reforms

(b) Ganga Action Plan

(c) linking of rivers

(d) protection of Western Ghats

Answer . d

44. Consider the following :

1. Calcutta Unitarian Committee

2. Tabernacle of New Dispensation

3. Indian Reform Association

Keshab Chandra Sen is associated with the establishment of which of the above?

(a) 1 and 3 only

(b) 2 and 3 only

(c) 3 only

(d) 1, 2 and 3

Answer . b

45. Which of the following is not a member of `Gulf Cooperation Council'?

(a) Iran

(b) Saudi Arabia

(c) Oman

(d) Kuwait

Answer . a

46. What is/are the purpose/purposes of Government's 'Sovereign Gold Bond

Scheme' and 'Gold Monetization Scheme'?

1. To bring the idle gold lying with Indian households into the economy

2. To promote FDI in the gold and jewellery sector

3. To reduce India's dependence on gold imports

Select the correct answer using the code given below.

(a) 1 only

(b) 2 and 3 only

(c) 1 and 3 only

(d) 1, 2 and 3

Answer . c

47. 'Belt and Road Initiative' is sometimes mentioned in the news in the context

of the affairs of

(a) African Union

(b) Brazil

(c) European Union

(d) China

Answer . d

48. Pradhan Mantri MUDRA Yojana is aimed at

(a) bringing the small entrepreneurs into formal financial system

(b) providing loans to poor farmers for cultivating particular crops

(c) providing pensions to old and destitute persons

(d) funding the voluntary organizations involved in the promotion of skill development

and employment generation

Answer . a

49. In which of the following regions of India are shale gas resources found?

1. Cambay Basin

2. Cauvery Basin

3. KrishnaGodavari

Basin

Select the correct answer using the code given below.

(a) 1 and 2 only

(b) 3 only

(c) 2 and 3 only

(d) 1, 2 and 3

Answer . d

50. 'Global Financial Stability Report' is prepared by the

(a) European Central Bank

(b) International Monetary Fund

(c) International Bank for Reconstruction and Development

(d) Organization for Economic Cooperation and Development

Answer . b

51. Regarding 'Atal Pension Yojana', which of the following statements is/are

correct?

1. It is a minimum guaranteed pension scheme mainly targeted at unorganized sector

workers.

2. Only one member of a family can join the scheme.

3. Same amount of pension is guaranteed for the spouse for life after subscriber's

death.

Select the correct answer using the code given below.

(a) 1 only

(b) 2 and 3 only

(c) 1 and 3 only

(d) 1, 2 and 3

Answer . c

52. The term 'Regional Comprehensive Economic Partnership' often appears in

the news in the context of the affairs of a group of countries known as

(a) G20

(b) ASEAN

(c) SCO

(d) SAARC

Answer . b

53. On which of the following can you find the Bureau of Energy Efficiency Star

Label?

1. Ceiling fans

2. Electric geysers

3. Tubular fluorescent lamps

Select the correct answer using the code given below.

(a) 1 and 2 only

(b) 3 only

(c) 2 and 3 only

(d) 1, 2 and 3

Answer . d

54. India is an important member of the 'International Thermonuclear
Experimental Reactor'. If this experiment succeeds, what is the immediate
advantage for India?

(a) It can use thorium in place of uranium for power generation

(b) It can attain a global role in satellite navigation

(c) It can drastically improve the efficiency of its fission reactors in power generation

(d) It can build fusion reactors for power generation

Answer . d

55. In the context of the history of India, consider the following pairs:

Term Description

(1) Eripatti : Land, revenue from which was set apart for the main¬tenance of the
village tank

(2) Taniyurs : Villages donated to a single Brahmin or a group of Brahmins

(3) Ghatikas : Colleges generally attached to the temples

Which of the pairs given above is/are correctly matched?

(a) 1 and 2

(b) 3 only

(c) 2 and 3

(d) 1 and 3

Answer . d

56. Consider the following statements:

(1) The International Solar Alliance was launched at the United Nations Climate Change
Conference in 2015.

(2) The Alliance includes all the member countries of the United Nations.

Which of the statements given above is/are correct?

(a) 1 only

(b) 2 only

(c) Both 1 and 2

(d) Neither 1 nor 2

Answer . a

57. 'European Stability Mechanism', sometimes seen in the news, is an

(a) agency created by EU to deal with the impact of millions of refugees arriving from

Middle East

(b) agency of EU that provides financial assistance to eurozone countries

(c) agency of EU to deal with all the bilateral and multilateral agreements on trade

(d) agency of EU to deal with the conflicts arising among the member countries

Answer . b

58. Which of the following is/are the advantage /advantages of practising drip

irrigation?

1. Reduction in weed

2. Reduction in soil salinity

3. Reduction in soil erosion

Select the correct answer using the code given below.

(a) 1 and 2 only

(b) 3 only

(c) 1 and 3 only

(d) None of the above is an advantage of practising drip irrigation

Answer . c

59. Regarding DigiLocker', sometimes seen in the news, which of the following

statements is/are correct?

1 It is a digital locker system offered by the Government under Digital India Programme.

2. It allows you to access your edocuments

irrespective of your physical location.

Select the correct answer using the code given below.

(a) 1 only

(b) 2 only

(c) Both 1 and 2

(d) Neither 1 nor 2

Answer . c

60. Recently, linking of which of the following rivers was undertaken?

(a) Cauvery and Tungabhadra

(b) Godavari and Krishna

(c) Mahanadi and Sone

(d) Narmada and Tapti

Answer . b

61. In the cities of our country, which among the following atmospheric gases are

normally considered in calculating the value of Air Quality Index?

1. Carbon dioxide

2. Carbon monoxide

3. Nitrogen dioxide

4. Sulfur dioxide

5. Methane

Select the correct answer using the code given below.

(a) 1, 2 and 3 only

(b) 2, 3 and 4 only

(c) 1, 4 and 5 only

(d) 1, 2, 3, 4 and 5

Answer . b

62. With reference to 'Astrosat', the astronomical observatory launched by India, which of the following statements is/are correct?

1. Other than USA and Russia, India is the only country to have launched a similar observatory into space.

2. Astrosat is a 2000 kg satellite placed in an orbit at 1650 km above the surface of the Earth.

Select the correct answer using the code given below.

(a) 1 only

(b) 2 only

(c) Both 1 and 2

(d) Neither 1 nor 2

Answer . a

63. With reference to the economic history of medieval India, the term Araghatta' refers to

(a) bonded labour

(b) land grants made to military officers

(c) waterwheel used in the irrigation of land

(d) wastel and converted to cultivated land

Answer . c

64. With reference to the cultural history of India, the memorizing of chronicles, dynastic histories and Epictales was the profession of who of the following?

(a) Shramana

(b) Parivraaj a k a

(c) Agrahaarika

(d) Maagadha

Answer .d

65. Recently, for the first time in our country, which of the following States has declared a particular butterfly as 'State Butterfly'?

(a) Arunachal Pradesh

(b) Himachal Pradesh

(c) Karnataka

(d) Maharashtra

Answer . d

66. Consider the following statements:

The Mangalyaan launched by ISRO

1. is also called the Mars Orbiter Mission

2. made India the second country to have a spacecraft orbit the Mars after USA

3. made India the only country to be successful in making its spacecraft orbit the Mars in its very first attempt

Which of the statements given above is/are correct?

(a) 1 only

(b) 2 and 3 only

(c) 1 and 3 only

(d) 1, 2 and 3

Answer .c

67. What was the main reason for the split in the Indian National Congress at Surat in 1907?

(a) Introduction of communalism into Indian politics by Lord Minto

(b) Extremists' lack of faith in the capacity of the moderates to negotiate with the British Government

(c) Foundation of Muslim League

(d) Aurobindo Ghosh's inability to be elected as the President of the Indian National Congress

Answer b

68. The plan of Sir Stafford Cripps envisaged that after the Second World War

(a) India should be granted complete independence(b) India should be partitioned into

two before granting independence

(c) India should be made a republic with the condition that she will join the

Commonwealth

(d) India should be given Dominion status

Answer .d

69. Consider the following pairs:

Famous place Region

1. Bodhgaya Baghelkhand

2. Khajuraho Bundelkhand

3. Shirdi Vidarbha

4. Nasik (Nashik) Malwa

5. Tirupati Rayalaseema

Which of the pairs given above are correctly matched?

(a) 1, 2 and 4

(b) 2, 3, 4 and 5

(c) 2 and 5 only

(d) 1, 3, 4 and 5

Answer .c

70. The Parliament of India acquires the power to legislate on any item in the

State List in the national interest if a resolution to thateffect is passed by the

(a) Lok Sabha by a simple majority of its total membership

(b) Lok Sabha by a majority of not less than twothirds

of its total membership

(c) Rajya Sabha by a simple majority of its total membership

(d) Rajya Sabha by a majority of not less than twothirds

of its members present and

voting

Answer .d

71. Recently, which of the following States has explored the possibility of

constructing an artificial inland port to be connected to sea by a long

navigational channel?

(a) Andhra Pradesh

(b) Chhattisgarh

(c) Karnataka

(d) Rajasthan

Answer .d

72. With reference to the Agreement at the UNFCCC Meeting in Paris in 2015,

which of the following statements is/are correct?

1. The Agreement was signed by all the member countries of the UN and it will go into

effect in 2017.

2. The Agreement aims to limit the greenhouse gas emissions so that the rise in

average global temperature by the end of this century does not exceed 2 °C or even 1.5

°C above preindustrial

levels.

3. Developed countries acknowledged their historical responsibility in global warming

and committed to donate $ 1000 billion a year from 2020 to help developing countries to

cope with climate change.

Select the correct answer using the code given below.

(a) 1 and 3 only

(b) 2 only

(c) 2 and 3 only

(d) 1, 2 and 3

Answer . b

73. Consider the following statements:

1. The Sustainable Development Goals were first proposed in 1972 by a global think tank called the 'Club of Rome'.

2. The Sustainable Development Goals have to be achieved by 2030.

Which of the statements given above is/are correct?

(a) 1 only

(b) 2 only

(c) Both 1 and 2

(d) Neither 1 nor 2

Answer. b

74. A recent movie titled The Man Who Knew Infinity is based on the biography of

(a) S. Ramanujan

(b) S. Chandrasekhar

(c) S. N. Bose

(d) C. V. Raman

Answer. a

75. Consider the following statements:

1. The minimum age prescribed for any person to be a member of Panchayat is 25 years.

2. A Panchayat reconstituted after premature dissolution continues only for the remainder period.

Which of the statements given above is/are correct?

(a) 1 only

(b) 2 only

(c) Both 1 and 2

(d) Neither 1 nor 2

Answer.d

76. Which of the following statements is/are correct?

1. A Bill pending in the Lok Sabha lapses on its prorogation.

2. A Bill pending in the Rajya Sabha, which has not been passed by the Lok Sabha, shall

not lapse on dissolution of the Lok Sabha.

Select the correct answer using the code given below.

(a) 1 only

(b) 2 only

(c) Both 1 and 2

(d) Neither 1 nor 2

Answer.b

77. Which of the following is/are the indicator/indicators used by IFPRI to

compute the Global Hunger Index Report?

1. Undernourishment

2. Child stunting

3. Child mortality

Select the correct answer using the code given below.

(a) 1 only

(b) 2 and 3 only

(c) 1 , 2 and 3

(d) 1 and 3 only

Answer. c

78. There has been a persistent deficit budget year after year. Which

action/actions of the following can be taken by the Government to reduce the

deficit?

1. Reducing revenue expenditure

2. Introducing new welfare schemes

3. Rationalizing subsidies

4. Reducing import duty

Select the correct answer using the code given below.

(a) 1 only

(b) 2 and 3 only

(c) 1 and 3 only

(d) 1, 2, 3 and 4

Answer.c

79. The establishment of 'Payment Banks' is being allowed in India to promote

financial inclusion. Which of the following statements is/are correct in this

context?

1. Mobile telephone companies and supermarket chains that are owned and controlled

by residents are eligible to be promoters of Payment Banks.

2. Payment Banks can issue both credit cards and debit cards.

3. Payment Banks cannot undertake lending activities.

Select the correct answer using the code given below.

(a) 1 and 2 only

(b) 1 and 3 only

(c) 2 only

(d) 1, 2 and 3

Answer.b

80. With reference to 'LiFi',

recently in the news, which of the following

statements is/are correct?

1. It uses light as the medium for highspeed

data transmission.

2. It is a wireless technology and is several times faster than 'WiFi'.

Select the correct answer using the code given below.

(a) 1 only

(b) 2 only

(c) Both 1 and 2

(d) Neither 1 nor 2

Answer.c

81. The term 'Intended Nationally Determined Contributions' is sometimes seen in

the news in the context of

(a) pledges made by the European countries to rehabilitate refugees from the waraffected

Middle East

(b) plan of action outlined by the countries of the world to combat climate change

(c) capital contributed by the member countries in the establishment of Asian

Infrastructure Investment Bank

(d) plan of action outlined by the countries of the world regarding Sustainable

Development Goals

Answer.b

82. Which one of the following is a purpose of `UDAY', a scheme of the

Government?

(a) Providing technical and financial assistance to startup

entre¬preneurs in the field of

renewable sources of energy

(b) Providing electricity to every gthousehold in the country by 2018

(c) Replacing the coalbased

power plants with natural gas, nuclear, solar, wind and tidal

power plants over a period of time

(d) Providing for financial turnaround and revival of power distribution companies

Answer.d

83. With reference to `IFC Masala Bonds', sometimes seen in the news, which of the statements given below is/are correct?

1. The International Finance Corporation, which offers these bonds, is an arm of the World Bank.

2. They are the rupeedenominated

bonds and are a source of debt financing for the

public and private sector.

Select the correct answer using the code given below.

(a) 1 only

(h) 2 only

(c) Both 1 and 2

(d) Neither 1 nor 2

Answer.c

84. Regarding the taxation system of Krishna Deva, the ruler of Vijayanagar,

consider the following statements :

1. The tax rate on land was fixed depending on the quality of the land.

2. Private owners of workshops paid an industries tax.

Which of the statements given above is/are correct?

(a) 1 only

(b) 2 only

(c) Both 1 and 2

(d) Neither 1 nor 2

Answer. c

85. Which one of the following books of ancient India has the love story of the

son of the founder of Sunga dynasty?

(a) Swapnavasavadatta

(b) Malavikagnirnitra

(c) Meghadoota

(d) Ratnavali

Answer.b

86. In the context of which of the following do you sometimes find the terms

'amber box, blue box and green box' in the news?

(a) WTO affairs

(b) SAARC affairs

(c) UNFCCC affairs

(d) IndiaEU

negotiations on FTA

Answer.a

87. Which of the following is/are included in the capital budget of the

Government of India?

1. Expenditure on acquisition of assets like roads, buildings, machinery, etc.

2. Loans received from foreign governments

3. Loans and advances granted to the States and Union Territories

Select the correct answer using the code given below.

(a) 1 only

(b) 2 and 3 only

(c) 1 and 3 only

(d) 1, 2 and 3

Answer.d

88. What is/are the importance/importances of the 'United Nations Convention to

Combat Desertification'?

1. It aims to promote effective action through innovative national programmes and

supportive international

partnerships.

2. It has a special/particular focus on South Asia and North Africa regions, and its Secretariat facilitates the allocation of major portion of financial resources to these regions.

3. It is committed to bottomup

approach, encouraging the participation of local people in

combating the desertification.

Select the correct answer using the code given below.

(a) 1 only

(b) 2 and 3 only

(c) 1 and 3 only

(d) 1, 2 and 3

Answer.c

89. Recently, which one of the following currencies has been proposed to be added to the basket of IMF's SDR?

(a) Rouble

(b) Rand

(c) Indian Rupee

(d) Renminbi

Answer.d

90. With reference to the International Monetary and Financial Cornmittee (IMFC), consider the following statements :

1. IMFC discusses matters of concern affecting the global economy, and advises the International Monetary Fund (IMF) on the direction of its work.

2. The World Bank participates as observer in IMFC's meetings.

Which of the statements given above is/are correct?

(a) 1 only

(b) 2 only

(c) Both 1 and 2

(d) Neither 1 nor 2

Answer.c

91. Rashtriya Garima Abhiyaan' is a national campaign to

(a) rehabilitate the homeless and destitute persons and provide them with suitable
sources of livelihood

(b) release the sex workers from their practice and provide them with alternative sources
of livelihood

(c) eradicate the practice of manual scavenging and rehabilitate the manual scavengers

(d) release the bonded labourers from their bondage and rehabilitate them

Answer.c

92. With reference to the cultural history of medieval India, consider the following
statements :

1. Siddhas (Sittars) of Tamil region were monotheistic and condemned idolatry.

2. Lingayats of Kannada region questioned the theory of rebirth and rejected the caste
hierarchy.

Which of the statements given above is/are correct?

(a) 1 only

(b) 2 only

(c) Both 1 and 2

(d) Neither 1 nor 2

Answer.a

93. Which of the following best describes the term 'import cover', sometimes seen
in the news?

(a) It is the ratio of value of imports to the Gross Domestic Product of a country

(b) It is the total value of imports of a country in a year

(c) It is the ratio between the value of exports and that of imports between two countries

(d) It is the number of months of imports that could be paid for by a country's

international reserves

Answer.d

94. Consider the following pairs :

Community sometimes In the affairs of mentioned in the news

1. Kurd : Bangladesh

2. Madhesi : Nepal

3. Rohingya : Myanmar

Which of the pairs given above is/are correctly matched?

(a) 1 and 2

(b) 2 only

(c) 2 and 3

(d) 3 only

Answer.c

95. With reference to 'Organization for the Prohibition of Chemical Weapons

(OPCW)', consider the following statements :

1. It is an organization of European Union in working relation with NATO and WHO.

2. It monitors chemical industry to prevent new weapons from emerging.

3. It provides assistance and protection to States (Parties) against chemical weapons

threats.

Which of the statements given above is/are correct?

(a) 1 only

(b) 2 and 3 only

(c) 1 and 3 only

(d) 1, 2 and 3

Answer.b

96. With reference to 'Pradhan Mantri Fasal Bima Yojana', consider the following

statements:

1. Under this scheme, farmers will have to pay a uniform premium of two percent for any

crop they cultivate in any season of the year.

2. This scheme covers postharvest

losses arising out of cyclones and unseasonal rains.

Which of the statements given above is/are correct?

(a) 1 only

(b) 2 only

(c) Both 1 and 2

(d) Neither 1 nor 2

Answer.b

97. In which of the following regions of India are you most likely to come across

the `Great Indian Hornbill' in its natural habitat?

(a) Sand deserts of northwest India

(b) Higher Himalayas of Jammu and Kashmir

(c) Salt marshes of western Gujarat

(d) Western Ghats

Answer.d

98. Which of the following are the key features of 'National Ganga River Basin

Authority (NGRBA)?

1. River basin is the unit of planning and management.

2. It spearheads the river conservation efforts at the national level.

3. One of the Chief Ministers of the States through which the Ganga flows becomes the

Chairman of NGRBA on rotation basis.

Select the correct answer using the code given Below.

(a) 1 and 2 only

(b) 2 and 3 only

(c) 1 and 3 only

(d) 1, 2 and 3

Answer.a

99. Why does the Government of India promote the use of Neemcoated

Urea' in

agriculture?

(a) Release of Neem oil in the soil increases nitrogen fixation by the soil microorganisms

(b) Neem coating slows down the rate of dissolution of urea in the soil

(c) Nitrous oxide, which is a greenhouse gas, is not at all released into atmosphere by

crop fields

(d) It is a combination of a weedicide and a fertilizer for particular crops

Answer.a

100. Consider the following statements :

1. The Chief Secretary in a State is appointed by the Governor of that State.

2. The Chief Secretary in a State has a fixed tenure.

Which of the statements given above is/are correct?

(a) 1 only

(b) 2 only

(c) Both 1 and 2

(d) Neither 1 nor 2

Answer.d